And Then God Said... Th

And Then God Said...
Then *I* Said...
Then He Said...

Volume Two

Copyright © 2011 by Celest and David

No part of this book may be reproduced in any form or by any electronic or mechanical means, including information and storage retrieval systems, without permission in writing from Celest and David, except by a reviewer who may quote brief passages in a review.

This book is not a work of fiction and has been intentionally unedited.

The book cover art was designed by God and painted by Celest.

A special acknowledgement for special people.

We wish to thank Tim and Mike, our computer genius friends, and our good friend Thor for the job they have done with all the technical aspects of taking this book from its manuscript form, proofreading for typos and formatting it into book layout for the printer.

And Then God Said...
Then *I* Said...
Then He Said...

Volume Two

This book contains information God transmitted to Celestial (Celest) Blue Star of the Pleiades and David of Arcturus. In this book God continues to provide pertinent information to benefit all people regardless of their preconceived beliefs. These are the words of truth and wisdom as presented to humanity by the God of this Universe. This information is relevant to the further pursuit of truth and the debunking of the illusions that so many people on the planet still cling to.

Included in this book is a chapter that God transmitted to Chako Priest. There is also a special presentation by the Master "Kato."

God Talk